Letters
from
Chickadee Hill

The Letters
 Winston O. Abbott

The Drawings
 Bette Eaton Bossen

Published By
INSPIRATION HOUSE
South Windsor, Connecticut

SECOND PRINTING 1979

ISBN Number 0-918114-04-7

This book is a companion volume to

COME WALK AMONG THE STARS

SING WITH THE WIND

HAVE YOU HEARD THE CRICKET SONG

and

COME CLIMB MY HILL

Printed in U. S. A. by The Pond-Ekberg Co., Springfield, Mass.

Chickadee Hill

Dear Friends

The hour is late — and this old house
is dark and still — only the occasional snapping of
the embers on the hearth disturbs the quiet of this
winter night — now and then a tiny tongue of flame
casts a flickering light across the shadowed room —
and then the darkness and the quiet return — to-
night Chickadee Hill is filled with the warmth and
mellowness that only an old house can know — a
house that has watched the seasons come and go for a
century and a half from its vantage point atop this
hill —

it is late — so very late — and another
morning is waiting just beyond the great hemlocks to
the east — I stir reluctantly and know that once
again a dream must end — so often I have tried not
to restrict my life to man's calendar of time — to
avoid the neatly precise rows and squares filled with
the red and black numbers of passing time — to live
beyond the twelve pages that are torn away one by
one without regret —

there are no lines and angles in nature's
calendar — only gentle curves that reach around the
seasons and return to the place of their beginning —
I have tried to live by
the warmth of summer and the chill of winter — by

the bright sadness that is autumn — and the resur-
gence that is spring —

and if I fail once more — there are rare
moments like this night — when I am able to reach
beyond the restriction of man's calendar — to touch
— if ever so briefly — the mystery and the majesty
of the changing seasons — and perhaps — catch a
fleeting glimpse of the beauty of eternity as it sweeps
across this hill —

and I am sure that you will understand —
that beauty is more fulfilling — when one can reach
across the miles and touch the hand of a friend —

won't you share
with me —

as the new year begins —

I have been accorded a
great honor — I have been accepted as a friend by
one of the other residents of our hill — our language
differs —

but now we know — that language
is no barrier to a friendly
spirit —

of wings and song

The year now past has been filled — as have all the preceding years — with the failures and triumphs of man — and to a lesser degree with the failures and triumphs of each one of us — and should I pause to wonder — I might ask myself if I have reached a better understanding of my own life during these fleeting days — and if perhaps I have — it may well have been because of the Chickadees for whom this hill was named some years ago — and to understand this little incident you must first remember that I have a constant need to be in touch with the intangible things — the things which somehow always seem beyond my grasp — and yet inspire me to seek a better knowledge of the meaning and the purpose of my life —

and it happened as I was walking across the familiar meadow — as I have done perhaps a thousand times before — noticing all of the little unimportant things which are so very important to me — the brown oak leaf skittering across the crusted snow — the ice particles shining from the hemlock branches — the silhouettes of naked trees standing stark against the winter sky — the brown weeds and grasses bending in tune to the rising voice of the wind —

near the ancient apple tree at the upper reach of the garden — I paused to watch the sunlight sparkling upon the broad expanse of snow — and as I watched — a solitary chickadee dipped out of the hemlock and came flying toward me — instinctively I held out an open hand — and an instant later the jaunty little bird lit upon my finger — searched me with bright and beady eyes — cocked her head to one side and

whistled "dee — dee — dee" — and then repeated
"chickadee — dee — dee" — as if by way of intro-
duction —

we have fed the wild birds throughout
each of the winters that have passed across our hill —
and yet this was the first time that one had become so
friendly — and in that moment I felt as if I had been
promoted — or possibly even graduated from the
confined and confused world of man to the greater
open world of nature unspoiled and free —

I well know that there are
learned and scientific observers who will say that a
bird sings to promote the circulation — or to communicate with another bird — or for some other very
obvious reason — but to me a chickadee sings
because it is happy — and because the world needs a
song — for I have always held to an intense belief
that every bit of song drowns out something of dis-
cord — every bit of kindness replaces something of
malice or hatred — and each bit of beauty erases
some portion of ugliness —

and now that I have finally been accepted —
a half dozen of the black capped chickadees will come
and accept the gift of sunflower seeds from my outstretched hands — and even deliberately scatter a
few about that the cardinal and the raspberry finches
may share — yes — I know that the bird books refer
to these winter visitors as "purple finches" — but to
Winston Abbott of Chickadee Hill there will always
be raspberry finches — for the very same reason that
a bird sings because it is happy — for that is the way
it needs to be for me —

goldfinches in their somber winter suits have

been mingling with the juncoes and the tree sparrows — and they seem little perturbed to have a mourning dove settle into their midst — for there is enough and to share — the solitary cardinal looks out from his black mask and turns toward the wind to smooth his ruffled plumage — even a nuthatch stops by to pick up a stray seed while waiting for the larger hairy woodpecker to move away from the suet feeder — color and constant motion brighten the winter landscape and add needed beauty to the winter world —

only a few days ago we had another visitor come to share our bounty — a plump and vigorous robin was searching for food beneath the sheltering branches of the hemlock — yes — I also know that there are supposedly sound theories and explanations as to why a few robins do not make their annual pilgrimage to warmer climates — but it also just might be that someone here amid this New England winter needed the presence of a single robin to carry the heart toward another spring — yes — you are right — it was I who needed it —

of course we know — don't we — that moonlight
holds no magic of its own — its power to fill the
night with dreams is purely of our
own imagining — or could we
be mistaken —

of winter moonlight —

The day just past was a winter day of many moods — tingling cold and warming sunshine — of gray clouds and blue sky — of encrusted ice reflecting the early morning sun — and at noon little rivulets of water dredging channels in the frozen earth — and carrying the miniature flotsam and jetsam of winter down the gently sloping hillside and into the icebound brook — and hopefully along the way bearing some of the seeds of autumn to where they will become a part of another spring — for all seeds are not given wings with which to seek their destination —

in the noon-day sunshine a pair of bluebirds came to warm themselves atop the split rail fence that has weathered to a silvery gray through the variable moods of our New England seasons — and their sweetly warbled song made the winter sunshine even warmer — and the sky as blue as the color of their wings — and I watched and listened with a deepening awareness that beauty is inseparable from life — and especially in the rarer moments when the human spirit reaches upward to gently touch the source of its creation — yes I know that such moments are rare and all too brief — but even this does not detract from my belief that this is the proof of the infinity of our lives —

for it really matters not in my relationship with you whether your concept of God takes the form of a person or a spirit — or a symbol of mystic power or the source of light — as long as we both know that we are a part of the stream of life that had its source at some level above the wisdom of man — and even

with our many differences of personality and temper-
ament can yet reach out to touch each other's
heart — when unexpected beauty lifts us for the
moment above ourselves and gives wings to the
soul —

this afternoon
I walked along the brook — and marvelled at the
sculptured ice that coated each stone with crystal
blue — sparkling with the sunlight in the open
spaces and dark where the hemlocks grow in profu-
sion — here and there I could hear the muffled
laughter of the waters — not the same gay song as in
the days of summer — but muted and softly gur-
gling beneath the burden of the ice — only in one
place did the waters appear at all and this was
beneath the edge of a broad shelf of ice — and here
green fronds were still waving with the motion of the
swiftly flowing waters — a sort of rhythm of the ele-
ments of life — for man could not exist without
water and air — and I for one could not exist without
the music of nature's simplicity — whether it be the
sighing of the wind — or the throbbing of the sea —
or just the laughter of a little brook that wanders
beside the Cider Mill road —

I stayed long enough to watch the changing
light of late afternoon transform the branches of a
pin oak into shadowy forms — and cover the waiting
hillside with a mantle of soft gray — and waited
until the first star appeared in the colorless sky — for
that single star is a symbol of the vastness and the
mystery of my world —

yes — this has been a day of many moods and
so has the night — for a little past midnight the sky

above Chickadee Hill was aglow with the brighter stars and a waning moon — and then slowly from the south an endless wave of cloud extinguished the stars and blurred the yellow of the moon into a dim and frosty light — much as if an unseen curtain was being drawn across the heaven by unseen hands — and as the moon slipped toward the horizon — the soft light spread across the winter hills — and made a path of gold that filled the windows of the house with a diffused radiance that beggars description —

and if you were awake at this late hour — perhaps you also shared this loveliness — and if you were not — perhaps you were gently touched with its beauty as you slept — for beauty is ever a part of beauty — as life is ever a part of life —

of course you know that the moonlight has no magic of its own — its power to fill the night with dreams is of course purely of our own imagining —

or could we be mistaken —

to-night —
        I listened to the soughing of the
wind in the hemlocks along the old stone wall —
        and felt my heart responding to
        the music of the world about me —

voices of the wind —

To-night there is something of the sound of spring in the voice of the wind — even though some snow is lingering over the sloping meadow of Chickadee Hill — and the stars are buried in a sea of gray and billowing cloud — for the voice of the wind has lost it harsh and discordant tone and is acquiring a tone of gentleness and yearning — and to one who has watched the changing seasons with wonder and humility — this is not too difficult to understand — for while I am aware that each succeeding year moves with quickening pace — yet I find my eager heart reaching for the spring with even greater impatience than a season ago —

to-night the voice of the wind has dwindled to a querulous cry — a soft whimpering not unlike a puppy dreaming in contented sleep — it is a friendly sound calling to the 'peepers' for a confirmation that spring is just a few days down the road — and assuring the winter sleepers that snowdrops are pushing upward through the lingering snow — there is a softness to the night — a promise of warming earth and brightening skies —

but I remember only a few short days ago when this same wind rattled the blinds on this old house with frenzied fury — and screamed defiantly down the great stone chimney — and hurled windfuls of sleet against the lighted windows — while I was dreaming of man's feeble strength pitted against the greater forces of nature — and yet appreciative that I could find peace amid the blustering fury of a winter storm — a peace that came of the understanding of the affinity of nature with all of life —

but I also remember walking out into the night after the frenzy of the storm had passed — and listening as the wind rustled the leaves of an oak along my path — whispered voices scratching little sounds upon the stillness of the night — and I remember the humming of the wires in the quiet dark — and the glittering stars filling the emptiness and immensity of space with reassuring points of light — for the emptiness and immensity of space are much more frightening in the total dark — and I remember as I walked slowly up the hill how the stars came down to meet me — and I hope that you have also shared such an experience — for mere words cannot describe the majesty of a star-filled night — after the storm has passed —

but the wind has other voices — the melancholy dirge that accompanies the sound of autumn leaves scurrying about in the darkness — the mourning lament for the naked trees saddened by summer's passing — for this too is a part of the music of life and another mood for another season —

and in the humid stillness of a summer night the voice of the wind can seldom be heard at all — but it brushes softly against the face with its cooling touch and fills the air with the fragrance of honeysuckle and scented stock — and moves on to refresh the grasses with gentle waves of motion — sometimes the wind sighs a little for the too swift passing of time — and sometimes sighs a little deeper that we are so prone to count life as hours and days instead of challenges and opportunities — only when a thunder-storm comes to cool and refresh the parched earth does the wind raise its voice at all — and then only as an accompaniment for the rolling of the thunder —

but to-night is different — surely there is something of the sound of spring in the voice of the wind — something that must be heard by the spirit as well as the ear — for it is made tangible by something that the heart knows to be intangible — a sensitivity to the great mystery of birth and life — of swelling buds — of growing things shaking off the dormancy of rest — of returning birds — of music in the marsh where life began — of the laughter of the brook — and very soon the song of the wind will join the rains to wash and cleanse the earth of its last vestige of winter —

and in my heart spring began to-night — with the soughing of the wind in the hemlocks along the old stone wall — all of these things I know that you have shared with me — for we have walked together through the days of winter —

and we shall walk to-gether toward a bright to-morrow —

have you ever watched a
Mourning Cloak fanning its
cramped wings in the April
sunshine —
         there is so much
to learn of strength — from
fragile things —

a time of expectations —

There are many invaluable things that I have learned upon the windswept hills and in the quiet of woodland and marsh — and not the least of these becomes a lesson in patience and impatience — for April is a tease — and one has to accept her fickleness — and understand that expectations must often be tempered with patience — for I have been eagerly waiting for the song of the 'peepers' to release my spirit from the final and often lingering burdens of winter —

and this is the second year of the notebooks at Chickadee Hill that the March winds have blustered down the road and gone — without once hearing the opening chorus of the symphony of spring — the last few days of March were days of real promise — until a north wind swept out of the early morning darkness and left an inch of cotton snow upon the waking hills — but I mustered a little more patience and by midmorning was rewarded by a bright new day — a scintillating world of white — clear and sparkling under the warming sunshine — it was as if winter did not wish to leave me as an enemy after some unforgettable days in February — and I gladly accepted this gesture of good-will — for it was a soft and transient snow — giving indescribable loveliness to the mornning — and causing but little concern to the bright breasted robins that have recently come home —

I shared this scene of fragile beauty with a lone song sparrow who perched high upon a twig and sang — shaking little feathers of snow from

the swaying branch with the unrestrained rapture of
the song — as I paused to listen — bits of white
drifted down upon me — and the tiny crystals
sparkled for an instant in the sunlight and were gone
— and I could not help but think of the many things
of beauty that last but a second against the great im
mensity of time — and I think that the spirit has
reason to be sad because this is so — because the
needs of the spirit are many and continuing —

but this is a time for expectations —
and I must admit that I am not always as patient as I
should be — for the winter restricts my enjoyment of
the fields and woods much as it impedes the flowing
of the brook with its icy breath — and so I am
anxious to look for the first green shoots of the skunk
cabbage pushing upward from the leaf mold — and
watch the fox sparrows scratch for food among the
sodden leaves — and hear that strange wild cry of the
geese moving northward under cover of the
darkness —

I need to see the first Mourning Cloak fanning
its cramped wings in the April sunshine — and see
the blossoms of the forsythia change the spindly fin-
gers of a common bush into sprays of yellow gold — I
need the warmth of lengthening days and the mellowing darkness of April nights — yes — I need
each and every one of these harbingers of spring —
and I especially need the first faint and wavering note
of those 'peepers' in the marginal pond across the
road —

and I am often impatient even though I know
that spring is not the instant miracle it appears to

be — buds were formed months ago and protected through the winter cold — seeds were hidden beneath the falling leaves and broken grasses — creatures large and small hibernated beneath the frost line — or wove silken cocoons to protect themselves — or burrowed in the soft mud at the bottom of the pond — certainly not from knowledge gained from living — but from intuition provided by the Creator in the continuing pattern of all life — and are we not a part of life — both you and I —

we do not know — you and I — what the pattern for our individual lives will be — but we do know — that there must be a purpose for our living — perhaps it is but to reach out to one who needs a strengthening hand — perhaps it is to lift the heart of another against the loneliness of life — perhaps it is to plant love where hate once grew —

surely we should not look upon the miracles of spring without remembering that they were once a part of autumn — surely we cannot look upon a single spray of forsythia without a promise for tomorrow —

and from Chickadee Hill — a wish that this may be the most beautiful ever — this month of April —

those who work upon the land — know the
touch of elemental things —
                                    the
spiritual value of honest toil —

of stone walls and sunsets —

Tell me — just where has April gone — April with her smiling skies and sudden showers — fickle lady of spring who silenced the peepers with a sheet of ice upon the pond on Saturday — and sent the thermometer soaring into the sixties on Sunday — April who in her whimsical way chased winter from our hill with days of golden sunshine — and then laughingly spilled three inches of water upon us in three days — but she has gone — and May has come to take her place — and to-night the hill is ringing with the love songs of the peepers — and I am sitting by the west window watching the last pinks and golds of the sunset settle upon the ancient stone wall that rambles along the meadow's edge —

and in another few moments the splendor of the evening sky will have faded into the darkness — but the permanence and strength of the old wall remains as it has for a hundred years upon the land — for it was laid stone upon stone by the strength of the men who lived and worked close to the fertile earth —

and as dusk is a time for musing and for remembering — perhaps it is good to remember that stone walls are a part of our New England heritage — created of the necessity of clearing the land for more efficient use — dividing the tilled fields from the meadow and pasture — separating the orchard from the woodlot — created by the patience and skill of craftsmen who took just pride in their work — and who knew the spiritual value of honest toil — toil that was tempered and seasoned with sunlight and rain and the touch of elemental things — for how else could something of such enduring beauty rise from the common stones of the field —

and to-day the moss and lichen covered wall stands as a silent tribute to those men of generations past — who have lived their lives and gone away — and in their passing have become a part of the heritage from which my own life has been nourished and strengthened — for life is as fragile and fleeting as the delicate colors of the sunset — and yet as enduring as the endless miles of stone fences that wander across our beloved hills — for we must remember that in a few brief hours other pinks and golds will spread across the eastern sky — and the ending of yesterday becomes the beginning of today —

and in the new light of morning the face of the familiar wall will be silvered gray — and the unfolding leaves will clothe the meadow in a green mist — and a chipmunk will scurry from between the sheltering stones and disappear among the ferns — and scurry back when a towhee sends a little shower of leaves flying from his busy feet — and the wall and the two tall trees at either end will form a frame to hold the picture of beautiful May for all to see —

still other boulder walls will frame the fields of dark and furrowed earth — freshly turned by the plow and moist and fragrant in these mellowing days — while in the far corner where the wall bends toward the pasture — petals from the shadblow drift silently upon the ground — reminding us that but a few brief weeks ago this same

picture frame held dark blue shadows brushed upon
the white canvas of winter — and our ancient
boundaries were completely hidden beneath the
windswept snow —

                              but
of all the things of beauty framed by our rambling
walls — I think I love best the sunsets that light the
windows of Chickadee Hill with reflected glory — as
if the day in leaving had gathered all of the golden
sunshine into one last lingering flame to burn away
the weariness of the day — for twilight is a time of
peace and tranquility — and the dusk is filled with
memories as the night is filled with stars — and they
burn even more brightly as the darkness deepens —
and this we share and understand — because we
have so much in common —

to accept the wind upon one's face — is to understand the unseen things that brush ever so lightly
against the spirit — and often in the dark —

a silken web —

I am by nature a grateful person — grateful for ever so many things — and not the least among them the knowledge that nature provides some understanding of the vagaries and uncertainties of life — and for most of us there are many — her changing but changeless beauty helps us to endure the things of ugliness — her ever continuing struggle for perfection offers faith when it is needed most — her constant reminder that all of life is a continuing process helps to reconcile us to the fleeting days and years — and the incomparable loveliness of this June afternoon has the power to heal many of the ills of the body — and most of the vicissitudes of the spirit — and this dear friends is not just hearsay —

perhaps it would be an exaggeration to say that all aches and pains will vanish beneath the warmth of the summer sunshine — but I do know that there is a miraculous healing power available to all who will let the spirit become absorbed in the infinity of earth and sky — I have learned that the refreshing coolness of the rain can wash away the dusts of doubt that settle upon the spirit — and the summer breezes can dissipate the wisps of selfishness that often come between us and our better selves — yes — I also know — that not even nature can erase the many moments of loneliness that come to each of us in turn — for loneliness is the intangible cord that binds our lives to the mystery of the past and the greater mystery of the future —

and this very afternoon I stretched out upon the warm earth beneath the spreading branches of a huge oak — and absorbed something of the strength symbolized by a great and sheltering tree — for years ago — or perhaps it was even seconds in the immensity of time — this giant was a mere seedling struggling for a root-hold in the fertile earth — and to-day its outstretched branches cast a filagreed pattern of light and shadow upon the ground beneath — while hidden amid the foliage the birds find shelter for their nests — and it is important to me to remember that the life of this towering tree was once contained in an acorn that could be hidden in the palm of my hand — and yet undoubtedly I will continue to ask — where does one find strength to meet one's needs —

but strength is also found in fragile things — in tiny things — and in places unexpected — for over there stretched between the blades of grass is a silken spider web — woven in the darkness and patterned in geometric perfection — its silken strands as scintillating as a sunbeam — and yet with strength to hold the diamonds of the morning dew — and defy the sweeping winds that sway the great branches of the oak above it — yes — there is strength in fragile things — in the wings of the swallow that skims above the meadow — in the nodding grasses that bend and bow at the touch of the wind — even in the myriad whispered sounds that fill the listening silence of this June day with rare music —

and if I had not learned from nature that there is strength in tiny and fragile things — how would I have come to know that there is also strength in things unseen and intangible — in memories that

bring the rapture of other days into this present hour
— of love that reaches across the days and the darkness to light fresh candles in our weary hearts — of
the understanding that often passes without a spoken
word — of a remembered smile that somehow does
not fade with time's passing — of countless other
things from which the fabric of our lives is woven —
yes — we
shall find our strength where we shall seek it — in
the majestic oak that lifts its branches to the sky —
in the gossamer threads of a tiny spider web — but
even more in the innumerable unseen things that
brush ever so lightly against the spirit — and often in
the dark —

I think it wonderful — that man can predict the
exact moment of to-morrow's sunrise —
I think it even more wonderful
that the sun should rise —

I was thinking about a leaf and a star —
Too often — it requires the passing of much
valuable time — before most of us come to know and
understand that a leaf and a star are one —

I think it wonderful that man's curiosity
reaches out into the vast space of the heavens — and
wonderful too that man has walked upon the moon
— although I cannot help but think of the hungry
that could be fed — and the homeless sheltered —
and the underpriviledged educated with the money
that was spent in its accomplishment —

I am impressed that man can plot a course
across the endless miles — and communicate while a
space journey is taking place — I am impressed that
man can chart the ebb and flow of the tides with total
accuracy — and determine the exact moment at
which one season gives way to another — but I think
it even more wonderful that somewhere behind the
pattern of creation these things were made to come
and pass in an orderly fashion — for if the destiny
and order of life were left entirely within our hands
— we might have reason to fear the eventualities —
sometimes it takes
even longer to know and understand that the leaf and
the seed are one — that all life gives way to new life
with the same pattern of precision that permeates all
of creation — and the created as well — all living
things — even a leaf —
this afternoon I paused in mowing
my lawn to pick up a maple leaf that had fallen pre-
maturely from the tree — a maple leaf is a very com-

mon thing here upon Chickadee Hill — for each of the five ancient maples that border the road have tens of thousands — and none unlike the others — and yet each single leaf should be an object of reverence for the wisdom of the Creator — for each and every leaf resembles the tree upon which it grows — as often children resemble parents in a way that is noticeable if undefinable — the stem of each leaf is a facsimile of the trunk of the tree — and stretching outward from the stem are dozens of fibrous veins that are patterned after the branches — growing smaller and finer as they reach the edge of the leaf — do you not wonder — as I wonder — that thousands grow upon a single tree and all are patterned in identical design — each one glossy and smooth upon the upper surface — of different shading and texture beneath — and if you hold any one of them toward the brightness of the sun — the leaf becomes the tree even as the seed becomes the leaf — and the same infinite wisdom that designed my maple trees also gave the seed its wings — that in another year another tree may come to grow in the far corner of the meadow — where some day another leaf will reveal something of the wonder and the mystery of creation to another soul that has been searching — even as you and I have been searching —

this evening — possibly there is no connection — I will leave you to interpret this as you will — but this evening — as the shadows stretched across the freshly cut lawn — a wood thrush flew from the thicket beside the brook — and perched on the branch of the maple from which the leaf had fallen — and sang with increasing intensity as the twilight deepened into darkness — perhaps this was simply a coincidence — but I would be unwilling to say that this was so — for many unusual things have come at predestined times to strengthen faith — yes — I know that this could have been a mere coincidence — but it could also have been that I needed the beauty of the song — for there are nights — as to-night — when there are no stars visible above Chick-adee Hill — and the darkness is deep and ever so still — and rests with lingering heaviness against the heart —

I know that if you had been here beside me to-night — you would not have said that the thrush upon the maple branch was a happenstance — no — you would not have said this — for you also know that the leaf and the star are one — just as truly as the leaf and the seed are one —

each wild flower and plant follows the
pattern of its own creation —
                                        and
fulfills some special purpose in the
master plan of the Creator —

a cluster of yellow blossoms —

It is not strange to me at all — that an ordinary plant in the meadow should involve the mind in the mystery of life — perhaps it was simply that it was not growing there last year — but this August finds it holding a hundred yellow blossoms above the heads of the ripening grasses — I do not know its botanical name — in fact I do not know its name at all — presumably it is some sort of daisy — but really this is not the important thing to me —

it is important that it came to grow in the meadow without assistance from you or from me — perhaps seeded by a bird in a hurried flight — perhaps a passenger of the wind — in fact the very amusing thought came to me that perhaps it was a fugitive from a formal garden — choosing to enjoy the freedom of the meadow and the company of the common grasses —

a little farther beyond — where and old canal once carried water to the mills along the Cider Mill Road — another plant has struggled upward from the tangled weeds and briars — holding dozens of miniature yellow stars upon its slender branches — as fragile as the wing of a butterfly and as golden as the August sunlight — and as I leaned forward to better remember its beauty a tiny wren flew out of the thicket and reprimanded me for the intrusion — and I withdrew knowing that there was a hidden nest somewhere amid the security of nature's lavish protection —

and as I moved away from the tangle I saw a huge mushroom of dusty pink and above it a jack-in-the-pulpit that had grown at least two feet tall — it was only natural to muse on the variety of life that had found nourishment in the rich black earth of the old canal — each plant following the pattern of its own creation and fulfilling some unknown purpose in the master plan for the universe —

musing further my mind came to think of the various personalities and temperaments that rise from similar environments — each has so much in common with the others and yet unique in its own right — and I thought with a deepening appreciation of the many lives that have brushed lightly against my own — leaving in their passing some gift of faith and courage and something of gentleness — and yes — fortunately some smattering of wisdom too — and as it is a prerequisite to happiness that one should not receive without giving — I must remember that I owe something of courage to those who have been bruised and buffeted by life — and something of gentleness to those who have known too much of the hurts and the harshness — and something of my inner self to those who stand lonely and afraid — for I have received so much — so very much —

yes — I know full well that I am something of a mystic — and I have no apologies for being such — but I am ever grateful that I am sensitive to nature's blessings — the thrush that came to sing upon the maple branch — the blossoms of gold that mysteriously appeared amid the meadow grasses — the rainbow that stretched across the sodden hills — surely in answer to a very special need — and I have never thought it strange at all that we can communicate across the miles without the

sound of spoken word — no — I do not think this
strange at all — for on this humid August night the
air lies heavy upon Chickadee Hill and sleep is elusive
— and in the stillness of the night there comes a
familiar sound from the pond across the way — the
deep-throated voice of the frog — not unlike the
sound of a bass viol being strummed by some unseen
hand — and moments later from farther away comes
the expected answer in a lesser voice — and in my
half-wakefulness I find it difficult to believe that man
can speak with man across a quarter million miles of
space — and has not always learned to communicate
with his neighbor across the street — but sadly this is
often true —

     and you must remember that all of these
thoughts were born of a common yellow flower that
raised its gift of beauty above the meadow grasses —
only perhaps — because I need a constant reminder
that my precious life is but one small spark that glows
for a moment upon the face of time —

     and even its feeble light may well
have been planned as a beacon for another soul —

the seasons move in an eternal circle — and autumn
is the time when the fertile earth rests from its
labors — as the urgency of growth is diminished —

as summer slips away —

How very quickly another month has slipped away to take its place among our memories — yet during these all too fleeting summer days I have learned many little things that I did not know before — little things — perhaps important only to me — or perhaps to you — yes — the daisy that I shared with you last month has become a wild sunflower — and my suggestion that possibly it was a fugitive from a formal garden has been substantiated by an authority on wild flowers — it is still holding a hundred smiling faces toward the late afternoon sun — valiantly holding its beauty against the onrushing time — standing alone and unprotected at the edge of the meadow — for the neighbor who mowed the hay carefully maneuvered his cutting bar around it — and in so doing has told me more about himself than I could have learned in hours of conversation —

it does seem quite reasonable for me to assume that there are plants and other growing things that rise above the normal pattern of their kind — as some people quietly but steadily refuse to become a part of the conformity and regimentation that man has forever tried to impose upon his world and upon his fellow men — and if you are one of these I am on your side —

and only a few yards away from my wild sunflower a plant of Queen Anne's lace is brightened by the contrasting shadows that are now stretching across the lawn — dozens of similar plants have seeded and browned but this one remains green and perky — holding tightly to the

ruby jewel that is carefully hidden within its center
— it is only during this past month that I learned
that this lacy flower was also called 'wild carrot' and
that it was an 'unwanted pest' and nuisance to the
farmers — but I am not a farmer and so I will continue to look upon it as a thing of beauty — for
many years I had not known about the ruby jewels
that are hidden in the hearts of its blossoms — but I
found them one afternoon when I was wandering
through the woods and fields — for by now you
know that I have spent many hours seeking the wisdom of nature — for it is always in the immediate
presence of the Creator —

and in these same
precious hours I have slowly assimilated other bits of
wisdom — and have learned that one should gather
and preserve each thing of beauty and loveliness —
less the accumulated years become barren and sterile
— for life has three seasons and I believe that each is
important to the others — for we move across the
face of time with gathering acceleration — and deepening intensity — the present is the time for accomplishment — the future is buoyed by anticipations
and expectations — and the yesterday holds the
memories that are needed to strengthen and sustain
us in the present —

and as the
seasons move in eternal circles — one comes to know
that autumn is the time when the fertile earth rests
from its labors as the urgency of growth is diminished
— perhaps it is not unlike the treasured hours that
come before the dark — when the heat of the day is
abated and the moist coolness comes with the lengthening shadows — and the Queen Anne's Lace lifts its

delicate flowers to challenge the dusk — softening the darkness with its white blossoms —

and now —
in just a little while the softness of the night will hush the activities of the day — and peace will cover this quiet hill — as I wish that it might cover our troubled world — yes — in a few more moments I will lose the beauty of the Queen Anne's Lace as night comes down to cover the earth — but I know that the morning sun will rekindle its beauty — and I will remember the ruby jewel hidden against its heart —

for what one has found is never lost — and this is from wisdom not always found in the minds of men — but always present in the heart that feels the weight of a single falling leaf — and my heart does —

this is the month of bright
warm days and cool brisk
nights — of quiet birds
that do not sing —

The mists of autumn days —

This is the season of bright warm days and cool brisk nights — of quiet birds that do not sing — of tapestried hills softened in the early morning hours by mists that are born of the cooling earth — surely nature has planned these soft and muted colors as the dawn spreads across the distant hills — for you and I are not far enough removed from the shadows of sleep to fully appreciate the morning splendor of our incomparable New England autumns — molten golds and crimsons interspersed with the greens of the conifers and the coppers of the beeches — hills and meadows cut into precise squares by lichen covered walls and canopied with a blue that blends with green in a way that only nature could devise and perfect —

and over all of this beauty rests the quiet sadness that is autumn — and in the midst of such encompassing loveliness one stands alone and unmoving and comes to know that there is no longer a mystery of death — and no longer a mystery of birth — no mystery to the speeding years that separate the two — just an accepted awareness that life ebbs and flows in the same manner that the tides rise and fall within defined patterns — and of course this is as it should be — for the origin of life as we know it had its inception in the muddied waters of time's beginning —

I have once more tried not to live entirely by man's calendar time — but by the quiet and orderly turning of the seasons — for life which is not man's creation should not be governed by man's restricting hand — yes — I know all too well that of necessity one must live and work in a world of partitioned hours — but one's spirit can — if one is fortunate enough — look to the timeless stars — the dawn — the dusk — and the changing seasons for a better understanding of the fact that time does not pass at all — it is we who pass across its sunlit and shadowed surface — often afraid and often lonely — but yet never quite alone —

and neither are we alone in our understanding of autumn — for it is a time of harvest for all of the creatures of the earth — the bluebirds search out the brilliant pokeberry — the monarch butterflies stretch their restless wings and feed upon the milkweed — yellow and black goldfinches sway upon the blossoms of the thistle and help in scattering its seeds upon the wind — the squirrels gather stores of acorns and hide them in a hundred foolish places — where the forgotten ones reach upward from the sheltering earth to offer food and sanctuary to creatures yet unborn — so does nature perpetuate its kind according to their needs — and it is so evident to those who are fortunate enough to sense the balance of the world of growing things — that man once more has failed to understand and observe the simple and basic laws of life which govern all creatures — laws which create, sustain and perpetuate —

for there is a magnitude of infinite wisdom within each tiny seed

— and autumn is a time of harvest for the creatures of fur and feather — and for us — who often overlook the importance of the so-called lesser forms of life — until upon such a day as this we come to know that there are no lesser forms of life — just life of which we are a part —

perhaps it is one of life's anachronisms that we are allowed to see things more clearly through the autumn mists — for one's powers of perception are sharpened as the need arises — and it becomes apparent that the bright colors are not diminished in the light of early morning — but softened and blended into even greater beauty —

for within the hour the mists will slowly rise and vanish into the crystal blue of the sky — bright sunlight will shine upon the places where the shadows were — and green and golds — browns and yellows — will spill down upon the earth to light the pathway toward the future —

and we will again feel the brush of sadness upon our spirits — for we learn so slowly — so very slowly —

to walk slowly across a meadow — is to know
that nothing of nature
is commonplace —

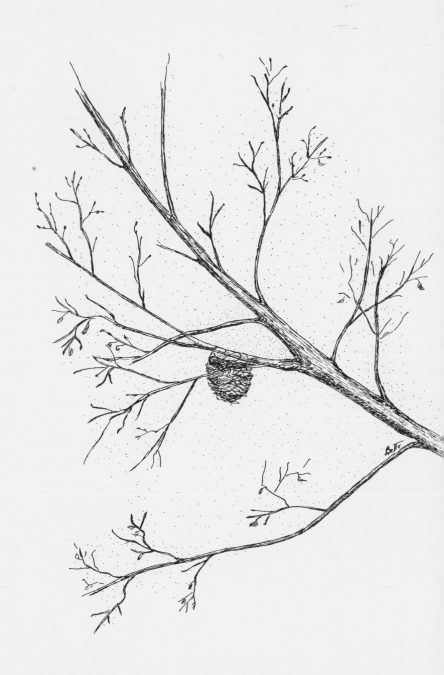

our summer residents have gone —
Any observant country dweller can tell at a glance that this is November — and without reference to that calendar hanging on the kitchen wall — for the summer residents have gone — and their abandoned nests are silhouetted upon the leafless branches of the trees — but there are also other ways of knowing that November has come again — the wind from the north and the west is sharp and chill and early morning finds the meadow brushed with silver — and even in the warmth of the bright sunshine one is aware that the earth is cooling — possibly it is the dull leaden gray of clouds that linger about the edge of the day — that tells us that the seasons are changing once again — and I find myself shivering in the late afternoon as little swirls of leaves scurry about my feet — hurrying at the insistence of the wind — and I find it most difficult to entirely shake off the autumnal sadness —

it was only yesterday that a dozen restless robins were gathered in the hedgerow — talking quietly among themselves — doubtless about the preparations for their wearying journey — and it was that very night that they left their familiar surroundings to move southward in the dark — answering some mystic or intuitive call — and I think it a thing of endless wonder that they can journey thousands of miles under the protective cover of the dark — and come spring — return to the very tree that now holds the deserted nest —

but many other nests are deserted here on the three acres of Chickadee Hill

— the hanging basket of the oriole will survive the winter storms and be there when the summer residents return — firmly anchored by its finely woven strands — for the oriole has chosen to suspend its nest upon the tip-ends of a branch — where it will rock gently to the motion of the slightest breeze — for this gay bird loves the motion of the branches and in the early days of summer its liquid song is as light and airy as the motion of the treetops —

and in marked contrast is the rickety nest of the catbird deep within the honeysuckle bush — capped with drying leaves and as forlorn in its emptiness as the deserted farmhouse atop Trombley's Hill — where the late afternoon sun reflects in a moment of glory upon the staring windows and is gone — I really believe that the catbird is fortunate in having its home last through the summer months — but I am also certain that the catbird could not care less — for this jovial mimic was far too busy exploring the thickets along the wall to devote unnecessary time to the task of nest building — and perhaps there is a lesson here for us — that some things are temporary at best and others are timeless in their values —

down in the apple tree the nest of the robin is wedged in the crotch between two branches — it will also fall apart during the winter storms and finally only a swatch of grass remains to mark its owners domain — and only a few yards beyond on a flat branch the exquisite thimble nest of the ruby throated hummingbird is blended with the coloring of the bark — and deftly camouflaged with tiny bits of moss and lichen until it appears to be only a knot upon the tree itself — what varied talents are given to the creatures of the feathered world — for each bird designs its own nest to suit its needs — and never to copy or outdo a neighbor — and I find this completely refreshing of itself —

almost beneath the maple a hundred drying stalks of the milkweed hold their seedpods open to the wind — waiting to release the tiny seeds when they can best be transported into tomorrow — in the slanting rays of sunlight the stalks and the silken floss are silvered against the background of brown and withered grasses — a common ordinary weed has become an object of beauty — and if we may stand here for a few more minutes we can share the ending of the day — and the incomparable splendor of a November sunset — with the clear yellow light of autumn streaming across the field and hedgerow — and making every stark and naked branch a filagree of dark against the light —

and if we will but close our eyes and listen we can still hear the golden notes of the oriole — drifting softly downward from the empty nest — for no part of nature's music is ever stilled — nothing must be commonplace for each and every thing that holds the gift of life has been touched by the hands of the Creator — as have you — and I —

there are some things that
    can be shared only with friends —
    this true story I leave with you —
    I believe that you will understand —
        because you are my friends —

I know that I am a dreamer —

but this is not a dream —
Again the hour is late and the fire has burned low —
the quiet of night is deep upon Chickadee Hill —
and once again the circle of the seasons has come back
to the place of its beginning — and another year has
slipped into the infinity of time —

this has been a year of joys
and of sadness — as have the many that have pre-
ceded it — simple joys of country living — and tra-
gedies which are the lot of all of us —

at the beginning of the
year I made a new friend — a chickadee who came to
accept me as an equal — and I was honored —

this year I have
lost a beloved friend — Thumper our collie of sorts
— the faithful guardian of our hill — who has
shared our happiness and our sorrows for fourteen
years — his vision and strength were failing — and
he did not see the car coming around the bend at the
end of the meadow — it was a great loss — a lasting
loss — and he left us during the glory of autumn —
and this is the season that always touches my heart
with sadness —

perhaps I should not tell
you this story at all — but you are friends and so I
shall — last night near midnight — I had finished
working at my desk — and as was my custom — I
stopped to look out across the meadow — the moon

was nearly full and the shadows of the maples made dark patterns on the newly fallen snow — only the sound of the wind gently rattling the shutters intruded upon the quiet — unexpectedly the lights of an approaching car shone around the bend of the road — and the screech of brakes quickly turned my gaze — crossing the road was Thumper — he evaded the car and trotted up the driveway — past the huge maple — and across the stepping stones — as he had done a thousand times before —

I grabbed a jacket and rushed outside — but the night was empty — but I had heard the screech of brakes — and there were tracks upon the newly fallen snow —

I went back inside and stood shivering in front of the dying fire — surely I thought — I am a rational person and certainly not given to hallucinating — and yet I had seen him — and there were the tracks leading directly to the kitchen door — I offer no explanation — nor do I ask you to accept this story — to me it remains one of many experiences that have touched my life with mystery — I am not one who will deny things because I cannot explain them — we know so little of the power that surrounds our fragile lives —

for another hour I sat before the fire — absorbing the warmth from the huge stones and musing about the happenings of the night — thinking of the stories this old house could tell — and sharing its mellowness with those who had lived here before my time — only a tiny glow remains of the maple log upon the hearth — the beginning of

another circle is coming over the eastern hills — it is
time for sleep and rest — rather reluctantly I placed
the screen before the smouldering ashes — and once
more looked out across the meadow — the hill was
covered with a soft light — and this old house filled
with a sense of deep and lasting peace —

I want so much to share it with you and with
all the world —

good-night my friends — and from
Chickadee Hill blessings —

Sincerely

Winston O. Abbott